ROADWORTHY CREATURE, ROADWORTHY CRAFT

Poems

Kate Magill

Fomite
Burlington, Vermont

Poems Copyright © by Kate Magill
Art Copyright © by Chris Gabriel

All rights reserved. No part of this book may be reproduced in any form or by any means without the prior written consent of the publisher, except in the case of brief quotations used in reviews and certain other noncommercial uses permitted by copyright law.

ISBN-13: 978-0-9832063-8-5
Library of Congress Control Number: 2011939154

Fomite
58 Peru Street
Burlington, VT 05401
www.fomitepress.com

Cover Art - Chris Gabriel
Author Photo - Donna Bister

ROADWORTHY CREATURE, ROADWORTHY CRAFT

for Jan, who taught me how to look at the horizon

ROADWORTHY CREATURE, ROADWORTHY CRAFT

Table of Contents

1. Felled   1
- This Song 3
- Bound 5
- On Loss: First Meditation 7
- Song For Little Foxes 9
- Sestina For The Villanelle 11
- A Poem For My Grandmother 13
- A Tired Haiku 14
- A Rain Peom, Not A Love Poem 15
- A Bread Song 18
- Second Meditation On Loss 19
- Rosaceae 21
- Notes On Identity 23
- Furnace, Not Inferno 24
- Inches 29
- Two Tobacco Haiku 31
- After The Ice Storm 32
- In Other Words 35
- More Notes On Identity 40

2. ALOUD   43
- Poetry Lesson 45
- American Cheese 49
- Falling Revisited 52
- Two Creatures Fixed And Fragile 55
- The Obsession Is Otherwise 59
- What Has Been Scattered 69

3. SPRUNG   77

- A Reminder 79
- For Sappho 81
- Taking Notes: Cold Comfort 82
- Still Snow 84
- Between Winter And Spring 85
- Eight White Tulips 87
- Monadnock 88
- On Being The Forgotten One 90
- Said The Explorer To The Settler 93
- May 95
- On Nomadism 101
- Spain, July 102
- Dead Tree 104
- Spinoza Poem #2 107
- Digging 108
- Because You Were Not Home 110

1. FELLED

What would the world be, once bereft
Of wet and wildness? Let them be left,
O let them be left, wildness and wet,
Long live the weeds and the wildness yet.
    —Gerard Manley Hopkins, "Inversnaid"

THIS SONG

The story started softly,
as we lay one night.
Beneath the cold crust, I told you,
there is music.
—Molten?
      —Perhaps it sloshes slightly.

Press to the earth an open ear
and hear the pulses hum up through the roots:
every blade of grass a megaphone,
and swaying daintily.

Now the cold crust grows.
The fallen snow is thick
and shifting,
breathing
like a lover
lost to slumber.

Do you want to lick
its earlobe?

Every renegade bit of sky
settles down and someday melts.

In the street,
the lamps lay down their orange tenderly,
like your hand on a lover's belly
sloping smooth and white.

Look not up.
Lift the stones
or look beneath
your own warm palms.

O, heavy heaven!
Jealous, the sky
takes the earth by the shoulders
and shakes.

BOUND

To begin with a well-defined image
is almost impossible. An island
might suffice. The bridges all eroded
or submerged, you cross by boat or by wing
or by will. You are feeling the distance,
the unearthly sigh of space as it gapes,
as the mainland pulls away and you lust
for some still thing, one fixed immutable,
and you're feeling the weight of your words stuck
slowmoving, nearly wedged among your throat's
pink headstrong muscles, words obsidian
and flint so smooth and toothed, the stonestruck tips
of long things waiting to be loosed. Deep out
among the ferns and fallen rotting pines
some quarry lies, a promise or a gleam.
You know stone takes to air to seek its mark,
your mark. Peel back the bark, you crouching one,
you dogfaced one. Your sorrow stretches far.
To look some other death straight in its eye,
its fishglass eye, is more than your own stone
eye, warm with sun, can handle. Build a pyre.
Leave the taking to the wind, leave the ripe
raspberries for the babes, leave the rotting
ones for birds. The birds will leave whenever
the leaves see fit. Birds free themselves over
and over. They enjoy the double pull.
They must. Which season is it you call home?
Which side of the horizon? Which corner
of this island? Places can be fickle.
A wise horizon I have never found.

Faintly lit ungraspables lie
always just beyond its knowing. Destinations
lead, mislead, and turn you loose into a
lone and loping wolf without a pack, with
little more than four paws and a tangled
burdocked pelt, a piercing moan, a low moon
leaving golden tracks across the water
rolling blindly toward its own horizon.
Huddle here among what's left of hunger
and brace yourself against the failing sun
before the shadows are too long to bear,
when you will feel the weight of more than words
or more words than any bones can hold.
Flickers of ancestral solipsism
haunt the shining pomegranate chambers
of your brain. What roots in sagging bentbacked
flesh is never time. Even memory
can't hold. All comes back to images,
erasure, doubt, a fragrance past recall.
Mythology is one more fallow plot,
and home is one more sharp wedge in your throat,
and what you thought was locked land is a road,
and you're wondering why all the older
folk keep telling you to stand up straighter.

ON LOSS: FIRST MEDITATION

You enter the woods with a vision
of the clear path stretched out before you.
The way is soft with loam and leaves.

Light seeps in, its angle sharper, sharper,
sharpening toward evening.
Branches filter out cloud, let gold sluice down.

You walk on.
The path you thought belonged to you dissolves:
coarse grain, dark and spreading outward, an embrace.

The path is moss, is dead leaves, is earth.
The path is roots and rises upward into trees,
exhales itself into sky.

You belong to it now:
lightless body engulfed by lightless path.
It spreads you out, blooms your limbs into a compass.

You belong to the four corners and beyond.
Your every breath becomes the sky,
a promise in leaves, and coursing just below the skin.

Owl cry; rough oily engine whine;
    rustle of small paws; a fire—
all is faraway and at your throat
and in you, smoldering.

You enter the woods as clay, unshapen and soft.
You leave it grapevine serpentines, hollows that howl,
etched as if with frost.

Rooted and aloft, you leave the woods but do not part from it.
Walking gentle into golden dawn,
you are the path you thought you'd lost.

Song for Little Foxes

I.

The leaves have gone from yellow,
slick like *papier-mâché* still wet,
to brown and alive,
parched leather skittering the pavement:
small animals we only dream to be.

II.

The little red fox was there,
on the white line that keeps cars
on the Interstate: stretched
and motionless, a pelt of flame,
still, unscathed and emptying.

Tempting me today,
as the morning before,
to pull over, stop and gather him,
curl him someplace warm. Something says,
He shouldn't be out in the wind and the rain,
he shouldn't be out in the wind and the rain—

I am not one to tell how bodies ought to leave.

I want not to take him
but to stay a moment
by his side, breathe his fur,
his flame, linger over
trafficmingled musk, shield
his body from the rush.

To stay.

To have that strength
instead of looking back,
whisking onward,
north, away.

SESTINA FOR THE VILLANELLE

Why is it I turn to villanelle,
obsessive form, longlost dance,
in moments ripe with grief?
As if to overcome the thing
I must repeat and repeat,
and ride the headlong fall.

Last year I lived the longest fall,
an endless end, villanelle
of dead leaves on repeat.
The winds leave flame drifts where they dance.
I dug in and found no thing,
the hollow after grief.

This urge to bare, to peel the grief
down to its brown core, windfall,
wormhearted, too ripe thing,
mealymouthed layers of villanelle,
manystepped circular dance,
circling toward loam, peat,

lichens and mosses. I repeat,
kitchenbound, paring down grief,
a bushelful, this dance
can't keep us from the headlong fall.
Not even the villanelle
will hold back this dark thing,

interior marshloping thing.
O, leaf after leaf, repeat
this line, this villanelle,
its spine, unbending bonestrung grief:
This is not my life. This fall—
Losing the steps— This dance—

I'm dancing someone else's dance.
Generations, layers of things,
unlusted, frail as fall—
Abandon them. Return, repeat,
there is no escaping grief,
this barren villanelle.

Snowfall, rain, bleak repeat:
the minutehand dance, toeing grief,
this thing not thing at all, but villanelle.

A Poem for My Grandmother

I've been trying to write a poem
about my grandmother.
I was wearing her t-shirt—
ivory, v-necked—when she died
and that felt symbolic,
like the plastic bag I stepped over today—
the long tube-shaped kind
they put day-old bagels in—
a long empty plastic bag
labeled "everything"
which I stepped over
only moments before
I was accosted by Mormons
offering me God
and warm unfamiliar smiles
just a block away
from the brick house
where my grandmother lived.

A Tired Haiku

Exhaustion sucks out
all the words and leaves stale husks
sapped of juice and rhyme.

A Rain Peom, Not a Love Poem

There is rain at the window
and rain at the window
and rain.

Mute clouds knock noiseless
and dull pressure muffles the skull.

Another sunrise to myself:
light seeps limp through grey film.
Another day of being inescapably awake,
unearthed and shuffling,
cornered by my own misinspiration.

It's been two years, I tell myself,
or three perhaps,
since I really, really wrote a poem.

My words and my words and my words
loop and break and hesitate back over themselves,
vicious, scrambling for meaning—
and there is no such thing.

This, the art of secrets and of audacious candor,
this spun silk thread, spiral meanderer,
this ripe flash in the right sun,
cannot be taught, only caught
by the corner of an eye, a quivering ear,
sung only with the breathlessness of wonder and of fear.

Why now do all the new songs come as echoes?
There are no words for love
that do not skirt and circle,
no words that do not hesitate.
Words themselves hesitations,
staving off what's necessary,
shrugging just out of sync with the heart.

To our lovers we offer up promises, starved,
husked-out hopes: the world as we wish it,
every word etched passages,
one long twisted route of escape—
root of longing, this language; we've learned nothing,
still afraid to root ourselves
in anything but premonition
or nostalgia—soil too dense to fruit—
tensed for the future
and tuned to the past
and blind to the moment
stretched out as vast
as oak branches on a blue day
to a child hunting acorns
who rests herself
        rooting her spine—notched vertebrae
        meet acorns
                meet pressure
                meet soil
                meet the moment, growing—
        while her eyes trace the lattice above her
        until all matter is line
        or space-between-the-line,
                all motion refers to blue
        or blue's shadow
and all blue is love
and all branches us.
One art for the damp earth

and for the parched sky,
I'll spend my days building
this latticework, fragile—

One art for peacemakers
and polemicists—
a latticework of
promises. I promise myself
I'll believe none of this.

One art for the runners,
for those who pick their way slow,
for the fern and for the rose,
one art for the secretkeepers
and the brazen—
one art.
One window.
One rain and still all too much,
one water, ceaseless, one glance
and one breath and one touch.

And there's rain on the window,
still rain on the window,
still rain.

And I can't get this poem to come for you—
not a love poem anyway.
All I've got is sallow and callous
and it's nothing to do with you—

it's universal, unrelenting as rain,
steady enough to wear straight through the panes,
sogging the curtains and swelling the floor,
and if I could just push it all aside
the whole day would turn so much clearer.

A Bread Song

She has about her that bakery smell:
cake yeast and salt and rising. Fall, she says,
is the season for baking. Crisp air makes
for crisp crusts. Her own skin is ovendamp,
ruddy from the fire. She stands tallying
desire: thirty-five whole wheat, a dozen
rye, one hundred and twenty-four baguettes.
Flour has pounded itself into her
fingernails, wound itself into the braids
piled and tied loosely under calico.
As she dusts down the calculus of growth—
scales, scoops, thermometer—she hums something
soft and regular, takes a cooling loaf
and cradles it, still humming, in her arms.

Second Meditation on Loss

My words leave me as leaves—
prematurely.
I cannot blame the frost.

I wake with sweat wooling my pores,
toss, roll, inescapable animal fecundity,
sharp musk.

Precious concentrate, thought:
once honeythick, raw, viscous and alive,
now weightless frass I cannot hold,
torn from me by gestures
not so strong, even,
as the wind.

I pass a bumpersticker asking,
GOT TODAY?
and think, *not really*.

Caught suffocating on the past—
arid grasses fill my nostrils,
wad behind my teeth:
everything a breathless scent,
deathsweet, rasping raw
all that tender epithelium.
My dear pink maw!

I stumble drunk on future
into brickstone stodgy promises
rest my head—the pressure—
choketongued, gaghearted,
bound with jute and lead,
rounding corners invisible,
swept by breath that isn't wind,
fearing the pop of chance bullet,
stray knife, window shatter,
first my limps go wrist.

Static crackles like thunder.
O, unfetttered, onslaughtered,
the radio waves! I ride.
Thought rides on thought—words not lost,
all breath static, phlegm stymies—
speech my parasite and I its host.
A perpetual standoff,
can't back from the brink—
Dare you to tell!
Dare all! Tell all!

Not words I've lost
but something hid too well,
strung taught as an arrow
and never launched.

ROSACEAE

Bitter as almonds
and cyanide sweet,
you walk as with nails
rusting under your feet
and you don't give half a
goddamn—
which is all they can say
as you trespass
        and saunter and slip underage
into bars   you are sick
        of the smoke and the salt
        and the flicker and buzz
        of the faces,
        one dying light bulb
        which you fear
might burn only between
        your sweet ears or the restless
wrought cage of your ribs.

You're carrying home roses
through the snow,
        you know who sent them,
        wish you didn't know—
blooms don't send you
anymore
        you have stopped dreaming
those hands   that name
doesn't ring in your far
darkened corners,
no longer wanders your halls.

You've turned loose
the whole herd
of what used to matter,
days now sand
through several sieves
and you have
        nothing left to give.
        You've watched your seeds
scatter and falter and mold
        in the grip of clay so heartless,
barren, cold, those seeds
        no longer yours to hold.

Whenever you say no
to the sun
or to some other unnamed star
        the sky hurls your word
        right back at you.

Whenever you say no
to the body you cannot bear,
the body whose love
        you've learned to fear,
        its voice becomes your echo.

Notes on Identity

I.

She says she will make something
and, having little else,
she makes something of herself.

II.

She has achieved the carriage of the writer
or of the ingrown toenail.
All narrative, all flesh, loops back upon itself.

III.

How sick I am of critics! You talk
of interdigitation. Please, just say
the poem laces its damn fingers.

Furnace, Not Inferno

This just occurred to me:

Poem after poem,
playing the hunger-search,
I penetrate the earth.
> *The earth beneath my feet*
> *the earth beneath my feet*
> *the earth beneath and how*
> *it hums up through the roots.*

Not once have I found Hell.
The underground, for sure,
is a fiery thing
in that here-and-there way,
not quite eternal.
We're far too real for that.
Hell works the surfaces.
It's in the dry stale heat
of boardrooms, factories,
the scorched black interstate:
shameless, flameless nowhere
places, where inferno
lurks. Not lurks! Bares its face,
parades, a ghastly grey
downbuttoned peacock, plumes
a disposable pride,
through opulent rooms hazed,
smokestench dependencies,
the deathless gloom of things
tied to eternity.
No more than an idea,
no less, forever clings

like tar. We breathe ideas—
not even breathing's free!
So long, easy laughter,
free will, unshackled speech!
So much for *Vogelfrei*.

*

Perhaps that's far too dark.
Perhaps dark's not halfbad.
Dark is the flipside of
that sun we've never had,
not yet. O, erratic,
endless revolutions
of the earth, of the heart,
of the centerless heart,
the earth that is pure core:
seeds and roots, fruit, leaves, all
indistinguishable!
That's the rhizome for you.
Grows in spite of the smoke,
drinks down the smoke with glee—
that must be the meaning
of Marx's *Vogelfrei*!

*

The earth grows from our feet,
or our feet from the earth?
Too much *telos* for you,
dear materialists?
How, then, to reckon birth?
And death? I want an end!
A nice warm bed of earth
and a story to tell
and a solid stone hearth

to look upon fondly
when I am dead and gone.
All those bloodborne notions:
sisterhood, brotherhood,
motherlove and fathers—
lambs on lams. How we love
and continue to love
all that is most hopeless,
fear those who go homeless
even as our homes tear
shreds and shackle the heart.
No other place to start
than that absolute *Yes*,
the glow of here, of home.
No other way to go:
from here to everywhere
takes time, never linear,
takes motion and muscle,
a sense of direction,
all directions: leading
outward, yes, but also
toward the center of all
centers, ever inward.
No other way to build
a fire but from earth:
not infernal *telos*,
this, it is a furnace.

*

So, we're playing the game
of spontaneity
and consciousness! What good
Leninists we are, with
our hours of talk talk talk,
deciding finally

to go with the gut. Must
be *the mysterious
curve of the straight line.* How
our revolution moves.

*

I'll never fall in love
like that again. I've tried.
It only happens once.
Knowing the unknown will
not ever be so new.
Notice how history
flattens us, me and you?
Cuts us down to *telos*?
Tells us that was true love,
what we had, but we let
go. That's mortals for you.
Always falling into
love and out again, and
naming what is not ours
to name. So goes labor.
I've been plucking apples
from the start, holding each
one as if it's my heart.

*

*Capitalism is
theft*. But then again, theft
is in some sense a gift.
Everything taken must
be given. History
may not be cyclical,
but things do come around.

*

For the determinists:

History's a given?
Oh, I beg to differ.
History is the theft
of past lives from our hands;
it gives them back to us,
datestamped and misshapen.

*

The body was, for once,
not a sight to behold.
We lay there together,
separate in the darkness
thicker than our eyelids.
Could light penetrate this?
Could our blunt memory?
Our minds dismember us.
But we're the underground.
We live beyond the eyes.

*

For once, a spontaneous haiku:

Fuck, even my love
turns into philosophy!
I hate you, Plato.

INCHES

> …we live by inches
> And only sometimes see the full dimension.
> Your stature's one I want to memorize—
> —Adrienne Rich, "Stepping Backwards"

You caught my eye one night:
a piece of beach glass on a warm shore,
a bright glance in a rough world.
I couldn't help myself:
my heart gasped,
tripped over itself gleefully. *So good,*
he looks so good, I said.
Because good, that solid syllable,
says more than well ever will.
You were standing in the kitchen,
so utterly quotidian, making pasta
and a vodka tonic, talking to your mother.
Watching you that night, I found myself
living through your vigor.
I was on the verge of burning out—
theorizing myself into oblivion.
You caught me that night in the kitchen.
All I could do was sit,
take in your movements,
quiet and astonished at your ease.
More than plain comfort:
you were lissome in your own skin,
full of grace and glee,
standing solid on your own two feet.
I return to the theme of integrity.
This is what I have been seeking,

in word and in deed,
something sure-footed
if not quite sure of itself,
reminding me
just how spontaneous the inches are,
and how alive,
weaving desire with need—
this is how I like to strive.

Two Tobacco Haiku

I. As Always

Incongrous night
of jasmine and cigarettes.
You fall asleep first.

II. Argument

Cigarettes inside
suck. But outside, in soft rain,
smoke has some power.

AFTER THE ICE STORM

Saturday:
I spend a solid hour quelling
this impulse to leave the bed—
        yours?
        ours?—
flip a lamp, sit in its pool,
notebook in my lap,
until you open your eyes,
say my name or come to my side
and hold your palm against my shoulder blade.

I want to shake you awake from a distance.

I close my eyes over a brittle vision
    nearly dream
in which I stand over the black current
watching something, contours caught by moonlight,
slipping underneath the dock.
    I cannot name it.

Coursing parallel and just below this fitful static
is the fear: we have lost the early electricity,
settled into something dim. My skin grown so at ease
no longer belongs.

What would I not do to still this doubt?
Its wire trembles through me like a second spine:
I pitch to one side, to the other,
opening and closing the space between these bodies,
tracing some inscrutable line.
And you:

your otherwise sweet snores spilling
into the room's grey space,
you sleep with such gusto
without me.

So I hold myself tight
in this room the color of doubt,
in this house too immaculate to belong to me,
this house in which I may or may not be long.
I hold myself quite still,
      as still as I can,
hoping that the coursing will subside,
that sleep will rise and morning come
to pull this impulse from me,
hoping most of all that you will hold me
with the hunger I've come to expect.

I tell myself I will not grasp,
will not cling as if life depends.
I am no small ungainly urchin
on a saltdashed rock.

I tell myself I must stand silent on the dock,
my blank pages open to catch what passes,
      name it.
      And if I dip a hand I will let myself be startled
by what slips between the fingers.

Outside, ice clings to branches
making broken music.
Here, your breath has softened,
steadied, you are still.

And I am still awake: awake and still,
softening toward morning, waiting
not for any precious sigh or word,
but for skin—
              yours?
                        ours?
to become unambiguous again.

IN OTHER WORDS

I.

We have grown competitive, this poem and I.

    We wake up together.
We eye one another.
      I'm going to kick your ass,
I say to it.

    And it simply grins:
not the gaping maw of a blank page,
but a toothy disarray, so many fractured phrases,
poorly parsed, halfarsed, a month's worth
of scattered text, tenpoint, singlespaced,
vague punctuation, rife with slant rhyme, faint assonance,
no manicure on this one. No make-up.
Unhemmed, shambling, stray hairs and a tattered sweater,
never does the dishes:
      a philosopher through and through, this poem.

      Or a poet.

II.

You draw a distinction I don't understand
between the philosopher and the artist.
    It startles me.
You reveal to me my tendency
      to conflate the two,
my desire to breathe art into theory,
        theory into art.

Is this my inner utilitarian?
To imagine all is driven by a singular need:

a place to set one's feet,
a way of laying claim
if not to life
at least to its terrain,
to eke out a scrap
of certitude
from between the teeth.

III.

I wake up alongside you,
prosey today, not prosebound or prosaic,
thinking in fullfledged sentences,
the sort that deserve to live in novels.
Seems I've forgotten them all.

The Leninist hesitates with supreme confidence.

A sudden lust for narrative:
I have things to say
that poetry cannot,
I don't know how to lift them.
Such stones! They won't be turned.
I have not the muscle—
      or the guts.

Since when is clarity so heavy?
What lives in the belly of what goes unsaid?
Last night, I tossed and tossed myself
out of sleep, chilled and fretting
over your new hesitations,

      splendid hesitations!
      Necessary deaths,
      uncalled-for hauntings.

Queasy with theory, not nearly awake,
scrambling for scraps of certitude,
      I hold myself so still.

> *The world does not need any more halfassed leftist academic equivocators. It needs genuine, generous, passionate souls. Fuck preponderance, fuck circumspection. You care too much to let go altogether.*

I say it without speaking it and wonder to myself,
which one of us is you?

It breaks me up, continuing to care.
And care is all that's holding me together.
I haven't found the knack for letting go.

Self-evident, these days,
to say the times are changing,
we the changelings,
not quite monsters,
but mixdreamed and impure.

If I say just one new thing,
unheard-of to whoever listens,
it will be enough.

This is where ambivalence begins.
Does survival ask another world
or simply for this one to listen?
      Not so simple as it seems.

I am after a trace,
a leaf saved,
                pressed between pages,
     more fragile than lace,
more like the dust on a doily.

       I find myself,
       over and over,
       in other people's words.

Maybe in love I'm just a teacher too.

My work is driven by this need
       to make some thing
              and give it to some body.

My work is never quite sated.

IV.

       Unhinged or uninhibited?
       It's getting to that point where I can't write

unless I'm doused and thoughtless.
I've got to stumble a bit
before the words set themselves right.

       Denying once again my agency—
       whither that good oldfashioned authority?

A matter of not crippling myself with questions—
the answers are only ever sketched.

>	We sketch ourselves in sand
>	to be smoothed away
>	by the wind, by the waves.

Most messages lost,
the bottle, the cork,
but the questions press and press.

>	What's left, what's necessary:
>	a suggestion.

I don't want the masterpiece.
I want the stutters and shrugs.

More Notes on Identity

I.

Your university teaches you
to be just feisty enough.

Your job teaches you
to hold it in.

Life shows you
that life is the feisty one.

You are an amateur.

II.

She can't quite let go
of the old bourgeois motto,
Make something of yourself.

A house is sticks,
a house is stones,

the girl is skin,
the girl is bones,

and a voicebox for a chimney

so the fire,
so the smoke
won't gut the rest.

2. ALOUD

Poesía
Perdóname por haberte ayudado a comprender
que no estás hecha sólo de palabras.

—Roque Dalton, "Arte poetica"

POETRY LESSON

As of today, I am officially
the most foulmouthed intern
and/or substitute teacher
the eighth grade class has ever had.
In the midst of discussing a nice little poem—
Ignatow's Bagel if you want to know—
in the midst of discussing the poem,
trying to give the kids a feel for it, I go:
    Oh shit! There goes my lunch!
And they dissolve,
every last one of them,
even the teacher,
    into fits.

And you know, it's the first time since I was their age
that I've been laughed at in class like that.
It never felt so good back then.

    And you know what else?

I think it really sold them—
    the profanity—
I think it really sold them
    on poetry.

Well, hell, I guess I'm just a pusher,
I'll do whatever it takes to get a few of them hooked—
and not on phonics.

I mean, nine times out of ten
you say *poetry* and you get some vacant stare,
maybe a shudder, a glimmer of fear.
Nine people out of ten don't want to hear
whatever it is you're about to say
about poetry.

But you say it anyway
because that's how poetry is played—
because poetry won't be taught,
won't be learned, just played—
half holy music, half convoluted game.
      And the best part?
      The poets never bothered
with writing down the rules.
They're too busy writing poetry.

Poetry spends the whole day staring out the window
as tiny birds chase sparrowhawks
and squirrels get hit by cars.
Poetry listens to everything the teacher doesn't say.

Poetry doesn't worry about winning arguments
but it starts them
and it stops them in their tracks.
Poetry does not give advice
and it does not give supporting evidence
paragraph by perfectly tedious paragraph.

Poetry gives you a box
swaddled in sharkskin
and tied up with grapevines
and when you finally get inside the box
you find
a grain of sand
or a bottle cap

or that word you never did understand
until just now.

I wanted to show those kids, somehow,
that poetry is not just some bearded guy on a bookplate,
not just Mother Goose,
not just red wine and black berets.
Poetry is plumbers and farmers
and bankers and bartenders
and housewives and pastry chefs
and housewives on the run.
Poetry is the loudmouth kid in the back row
and the real quiet kid up front.

Poetry is reckless people racing ramshackle lives
to the bottom of the hill
writing it all down while it happens—
they'll forget it otherwise.
And poetry is very boring people
living very boring lives
who write because there's nowhere else to go.

I'm wasting my words, I know.
I'm watching those little 13-year-old freckled ratfaces,
their eyes, as they learn how to doubt, how to mistrust,
but I can see the hairs prickling on the backs of their necks
and I know I'd better warn them now:

Poetry doesn't care about your wellbeing or mine,
poetry won't put dinner on the table
or pay the bills on time.

Poetry doesn't watch where it's going
because it's too busy
with its pocket notebook pressed
against the steering wheel

jotting down the ten perfect syllables
to finish last night's sonnet
so it runs a red light
doing 40 past a sign that says 25
and when it gets pulled over
all poetry can do is smile
all innocent-like, play dumb
and keep its fingers crossed under the dash
just like the rest of us.

AMERICAN CHEESE

I do not love him yet.
I love not knowing him.
He has the pure mystique
of a grilled cheese sandwich:
inside, I know, is gold.

He has that utterly American allure,
redolent of Whitman and Kerouac,
of vintage Schwinns, of genuinely faded denim,
glowing diners, dim bohemian cafés,
the yellow double-stripe down the center of the highway.

But American allure
is not American at all.

It is the absence of allegiance
that intrigues me. His past as I imagine it
is filled with labor unions, zydeco,
maple syrup, mailboxes,
chickenpox and mistletoe,
and a woman who makes sourdough waffles
every Saturday morning
and serves them to children
glued to the Looney Toons,
serves them with the fierce love
of a mother on the brink
of losing all her reasons why,
of drowning in the kitchen sink,
fears the morning she wakes up alone,
fears the evening she holds the receiver
and never hears a word past the dial tone—

It is the same in every home,
that's why I love him,
love not-him, love the history
I read beneath his skin.
America is etched into his bones—
but it's not America at all,
America is an idea and what I love
is the pure, warm breath and being—
not his breath, his being,
but it's there in him, so why not?

Why not nod and smile, and say *yeah,
I really dig him,* maybe talk about his eyes,
because it's all there in his eyes, which are brown and universal.
Or his smile, because when a person smiles the way he does
it is a mirror revealing the beautiful people, the ugly-but-sweet people,
the people who sing, who fix mufflers,
who knit hats for other people's children—
these are the ones I love! The many I love!

But what if I get too close,
stare too deep and idiomatically into his eyes?
In the narrow focus of infatuation
we lose our panoramic passion,
we forget the *we* entirely,
forget the bustling boulangeries,
forget to read other people's poetry,
forget the grilled cheese sandwiches—
not American, but fontina, camembert, havarti!

Or perhaps I'm just afraid of the plunge,
afraid the ocean will be too cold or not cold enough.
What if we kiss and still don't feel alive?
What if his tongue doesn't tear the breath from my lungs?
And does it matter?
In any case, it can't go on like this, we'll have to kiss
and say it's good or say it's bad,
tell people we're in love or not-in-love.

Never again will we have this intimacy we have now:
the intimacy of mystery, of distance, of imagined history.
And this is why it is impossible,
sitting in the coffee shop, talking to the girl behind the counter,
this girl I knew in high school who still pulls such a sweet ristretto,
who thinks she's asked me such a simple question,

this is why it is impossible to tell her
what's up between me and this guy
because it's not me and this guy,
it's me and the world—
but it's not me and the world,
it's the world alone, all there is—
the bread and coffee,
the grilled cheese sandwiches,
the way the slices melt until there are no slices anymore
and I don't feel so bad about my clumsy metaphors
because they are not mine, they're ours.

FALLING REVISITED

Why do they call it that—falling *in love?*
Sounds dangerous, she said, *like you could break a leg.*
And what's it got to do with gravity anyway?

Conflating physics
with the physical—
that girl's too goddamn analytical.
She's clearly never fallen.

I've fallen for boys in bookstores.
I've fallen for boys in bars.
I've fallen for the boy with the picket sign,
the boy with the guitar.
I've fallen for the boy with the backpack,
the boy with the bicycle,
the boy with the tattoos,
the boy with the glasses,
the boy with the Chuck Taylors,
with the Doc Martens,
the balding boy,
the bearded boy—
the boy in the bubble and the baby with the baboon heart
and I believe these are the days of miracle and wonder—
and I believe in falling now, more than ever,
I believe in falling most of all.
I believe in true love but not love at first sight
because love has so little to do with what we see—
it's chemical, it happens quicker than the eye.
If I had to, I'd say it is love at first breath, at first bite.

I've fallen for a vegan boy who loved to hunt
or dressed like a hunter at least;
and for a blond-haired blue-eyed boy
who learned his French in Africa;
and for a boy from somewhere near Barcelona
who made braided leather bracelets
and lived with seven dogs;
and for the boy who taught me
how to use a nail gun in New Orleans,
who smiled at me before I knew
he had a girl back home, a sweet girl
600 miles away, and who kept smiling
even after we both knew.

And I've fallen again for the picket sign
and again for the guitar.
Gravity does funny things to lovers
but I've never fallen quite like this before.

11:11: I come inside
after staring up just long enough
at that faintest of clouds,
la via lactea,
running roughly east to west
across the spangled sky.
Just long enough for my skin
to spangle with the first goosebumps.
It is the last full month of summer.
Just long enough to start thinking
how the oceans and the months
and all those long, strange, lonely stretches
between now and nowhere
are bound by the sky—
the one unbroken embrace.
Just long enough to wonder
why me and you,

how now instead of never,
whether this one is eternal,
or should I add it to the list?
I've fallen before
but never quite like this.

Two Creatures Fixed and Fragile

Oh, you—
with your salted swagger,
your appalling elegance!
    All I can do
    is stumble into you,
    all dry lips and
    hesitation,
fluctuation,
    imitation,
intimations—

                  You and I, we are
                  the wealth of nations,
                  yes—
            the flesh is gold,
                mind is diamond,
                heart is glowing coal.

You be the rubber
and I'll be the road,
you be the rubber
and I'll be the road,
you be the rubber
and we will be
        the moment
        road and rubber meet.

> *Your eyes damp asphalt,*
> *gasoline smeared,*
> *your mouth granite*
> *freshly quarried,*
> *rose quartz flecked.*

No casual passerby,
      I built the mineshaft.
Don't envy the ones
      who survive the collapse.
And I—
      flared, churning and slant—
never looked you in the eye
      and I never looked back.

> *Tell me your name,*
> *I will give you my heart.*
> *It's not much,*
> *I'm sorry,*
> *it's bitter and hard*
> *and as plain*
> *as the stone of a plum.*

Cannot call myself a woman
      and I've never been a girl.
Bristle at the ones who call me *miss*
      and *ma'am* is ten times worse,
at least, and I can't stand,
      can't stand, can't stand
people who say *lady*.

> *Tell me my name,*
> *I will give you my mind:*
> > *chambered, extravagant,*
> *seedswollen pomegranate,*
> > *lucent and ruby and sweet.*

Kiss me once, I taste of
ice and blood.
Twice, and I am smoke
and sandalwood.
And if you kiss me
one-two-three,
    I promise we will never see
the morning.

> *You and I, we thrive*
> > *on inbetween times:*
> *when the sky is neither*
> *blue nor black,*
> *when the body is a shadow*
> > *and the shadow is a*
> > *shadow of a shadow.*

    You be the driver
    and I'll be the deer,
    you be the driver
    and I'll be the deer,
    you be the driver
    and I'll be the deer
in your headlights.

> *My final breath won't be a sob,*
> *a whimper or a sigh.*
> *I'll sing for you.*
> > *Death is no more*
> > *than running out of fear.*
> > *The final breath*
> > *the sound of fury*
> > *satisfied.*

You take the pulse
and I'll be the ghost,
you take the pulse
and I'll be the ghost,
you
        hold the wrist as I rise.

THE OBSESSION IS OTHERWISE

I don't want you to worry about me.
I don't want you to tell me I'm beautiful
no matter what.
I don't want you to worry or warn me
or mourn for me
        when I disappear.
I want you to hold the hard parts and tell me they're soft.
I want you to bring me chocolates and hide the box
        where I will never find it.
I want you to lust for what is not here
and take what is.
I want you to complain about how my hipbones jut and hit you,
        and love it secretly.
I want you to hold me:
        hold me up to the light,
        and hold me up to the mirror,
        and hold me up to the camera.
I want you to tell me that I'm fat.
I want you to tell me that I'm right.

*

All these years and still
my utmost wonder is the hunger
manifest in words words words
and never flesh,
lists and lists
of what to eat
and most of all what not.
Thought consumes

and I devour thought.

I still don't know
how my self appears to others,
never will.
But I know how it sounds
in other mouths
so well I know the taste of it,
bitter, sour, so familiar
it's fermented now:
the worried, snide, jealous,
pitying asides.
Knowing voices
knowing nothing of interiors
speak surfaces—
as if all truth exists
across our surfaces!

I spent so long dreaming into a smooth plane.
I was a perfect surface, impossibly pure.
Thought myself impenetrable.
I lost and then I found and found and found.
Survival is to find the present and the past
live strung along the same silk thread.
If only I could be that line of spider silk:
to be liquid and then solid, all in one day!
The purity of form is in its stubborn flux.

*

I could tell you this is body image
but it's not.
It's pockets.   The earth
is all pockets.   I want—
I wanted—

       I wanted to whittle—
              I wanted to whittle myself
      into not-a-pocket:
something safe and clamshell closed,
      a locked line,
no suggestion of bulge,
      no point of entry,
a smooth surface,
a purity.

Only death is pure
and I'm not even sure of that.
There's no escaping gravity,
the endless rotund weight
even of bones stripped,
strapped to the earth,
trapped and limp and flattening
like dead leaves, like furs.

No girl lives wholly
in her limbs
          hair
         belly
     breasts.
Each finds ways
to resist her skin.

*

I went west. I left.
I dreamt a different sunset,
lost myself in my experiment,
lived out some farfetched legacy,
roadbound and lonely.

How selfish our notions of heritage.

I once said,
out loud but to myself,
canvassing a westcoast street:

History's the only way to breathe.

Words do not
bode the world.
Its mountains,
its swells of sand:
these are richer,
rougher things
than the mind
can understand.

The copses prosper,
glorious, resisting
all the machinations
of philanthropy,
reason and hands.

*

    Shaping surfaces.
This is how we pass our days,
how we whittle away what is
until we've nothing but a road,
    a dead line.

As if we'll find truth higher,
    deeper
than the precipice of everyday!

We've a knack for building emptiness,
  rooms not meant for living in,
scales that shimmer when they're dry
  and so we never swim.

Dealing as we do in teleology
  we call this conservation.

You like long limbs,
do you,
long and thin?
Like trees
planted narrow
by the paper mill
only to be reaped again
to satisfy
the whims of men—

I would mention monuments,
  I would broach narrative,
  introduce a problematic,
  indulge myself
  in being shallow and pedantic.

But that would be bald
without being bold.
Some days blatant theory leaves me cold:
  the same old stories told
  in too many weakspined syllables.

I'll be brash and say I'm not so gullible.
I know what school is doing to me,
I know its levels,
nothing left to marvel at,
they'll never say I'm level-headed—
a beveled mirror and a hello-there,

a smiling nod that means less than it should—

If we know so much
what are we waiting for?

Enlightenment?
A lightened load?
I can't find any dualism here:
My sex,
my intellect,
rolled into one agonized snail, a paper shell.

Hell is here.
Hell is the straight line
from the girl to the mirror,
from the mirror to an arbitrary number.

There's no line so empty as obsession.
Living fixed by this constant arrow
is not shame, not guilt,
but something else more subtle:
I will know it when I taste it
and the hunger cuts so deep
this bloodless line will satisfy.

*

All these years and all I know:
        not one of us is healthy.
We are obsessed, excessive,
puritanical,
secretive, indulgent,
self-denying, hyper-rational
        and critical in all the wrong ways,
tensed-up, overspent

        and falling apart and falling out,
seeking, seeking,
        self-indulgent and self-pitying
and pitiable, cold, remote
        and only outwardly articulate.

We strip our selves of passion and reflection,
we are nothing but reflected bodies—
other people's eyes,
        other people's eyes—
        We live, if you can call this living—
We survive
in other people's eyes,
not wishing to survive
but chained still by some salvaged grace:
call it instinct if you will,
a will with more rough courage
than the will we reify,
        deify,
        codify—
    lists— lists— lists—
and I am still in love
with lists.
        I am obsessed
with dollars,
        cents,
        and calories,
        pretending all the while
that I'm striving toward balance—
that fickle bitch, that myth
of eudaemonic middle classes
and their shamans—
but until I drop this burden
of counting every pleasure,
measuring extravagance,
I am possessed I belong not

to my body,
my body belongs not to me.
Fuck, why not blame it on the forces of history,
      economy and policy?
           Why not blame it on the media?
But this is so much deeper than the silver screen,
the black and white of text upon text upon lifeless text.

This is not Descartes.
This is not the rift between my body and my mind.
This is not capital,
what I sell or what I buy,
      not the clothes I wear,
the food I eat
      and don't eat,
or even the words I use
      to name myself,
name the world,
      blame the men
who made the words up
      in the first place.

      This is not a language game.
      This is me.

And I have never set foot on a treadmill,
never had a slimfast,
but I have lived on air,
      on promises,
on whispers,
      dreams and lies,
walking and whittling,
      whittling and walking,
      and feeling so alive!

I did.

I felt so alive
for a few slight months
before I utterly dried up,
before I found myself parched white,
illuminated in a way. I found a purity.
I worked down and down
until I found my bones.
I know my bones.
I know parts others are afraid to touch,
to even look at.
I know my ribcage
and my hips
and everything between the ribs,
between the hips.
I know what it means when the wall
between the man on top of me
and the man inside of me
is tissuepaper thin but strong and lithe
like a fresh snakeskin.

I know what it means to wipe all of it clean:
  a tabula rasa
  wasted
    barren
      utterly.

A desert: that is what I should have been.
They say women are fountains, pools,
merry brooks babbling—
but I had none of that. I was not
a woman, had no stake
in womanhood or even girlhood.
I was a body, half a body,
emptied and pressed flat,
the way you do with an old paper bag
before you store it on a shelf somewhere.

I was pure surface, yes,
and a pure internal.
I was within myself so tight
I thought I never would let go:
nothing left of me
for anyone to hold.

This is not a matter of beauty.
It's a matter of desire and a matter of control.
We all know beauty is a sham.
Control is what we're after:
suffering and power, hand in hand.

*

I don't want you to worry about me.
I don't want you to worry if I turn into
a letter of the alphabet.
It won't be a B or a D or a P—
nothing bulging, fruitlike—
a capital A perhaps,
or a little v,
something certain,
angular and slant.

I don't want you to worry about me.
I like it here, dissolving into atmosphere.
I like it. I like the hollowness. I want it.
I want nothing. I want you to want me.
I want you not to worry.

What Has Been Scattered

                    after John Berger, "The Hour of Poetry"

I.   The boon of language is not tenderness. All that it holds,
         it holds with exactitude and without pity. Even a term of
         endearment: the term is impartial; the context is all.

So this is where it begins.

      In this remote place,
         this dusty corner of the heart,
this island risen out of earth
I never thought to call my home—

Look now, you can see it curve
away from you, the earth.

I have eschewed the common places,
all the bland commitments,
the benevolence of order,
the well-decorated rooms.
I have clung to the outskirts,
the low roads, the fringes,
      and lo,
        here I am,
in the center of some solid thing
reeled round me without lock or key,
an island unmoved,
utterly,
        by wind.

      Out of the ashes
      of that hardnosed childhood

I have risen a romantic
of the oldest school there is,
in love with daffodils and hilltops,
with long kisses and with words—
the ones I never thought I'd say
and really mean:
I call you love,
        I call you home,
                I call you body bound to dream.

So this is how it happens.

We were not supposed to be all, end all,
take the cake and eat it too—

        You must be
        some deadly pleasure tendered
so perhaps I will forget
that what I'm really fighting for
is land and peace and bread!

But here I am each morning and I know:
these are the arms and these the eyes,
yours the only breathing body
strong enough to hold me down
for longer than a fleeting glimpse.

Some kind of energy that pulls me,
some kind of song that lulls me:
perhaps for once this center here
will hold all things will hang
in stillness merely breathing
'til the fire burns itself to coal.

II.   One can say of language that it is potentially the only human
        home, the only dwelling place that cannot be hostile to man.

A freak breeze, a quick squeeze:
I keep waiting for some one of us
to up and disappear. One year,
another year, all limbs still present,
still accentuated by each touch,
all traced, retraced, embraced,
we sleep and wake all ways in grace
but never quite the same way twice,
the way our dreams—
        our limbs—
                have twined—
                        O sweet supine Terpsichore!

        A certain fragile poetry
        in this admission then:
        my heart no more
        a wanderer, a renegade, a rogue?
        I've anchored it—
                you've anchored it—
                        O sweet blue hidden cove!

It's no trick to spend a whole life roaming,
not so easy to feel everywhere at home.

        I warn you now:
I won't have my love
civilized,
                domesticated,
        tranquilized,
                exterminated,
        hypnotized,
                evacuated
        into sweet oblivion.

I'll only have love clear and raw
as wind on a ridgeline in November.
If our home is going to tame us,
only love can keep us wild.

So, we are different
from the rest of life,
      the reeling carnival?
      All dance along the same fine shifting fautlines,
from pleasure just one missed step into darkness.
Even the surest of foot all someday fall.

I am trying as best I can to abstain from all words
as I hold this fretful creature up to you:
my heart in outstretched trembling hands.

      Beyond all reason,
      beyond rhyme perhaps,
my love utters,
      unwordly,
a language I can barely grasp,
adheres to a meter that will not scan,
      dances a strange and uncountable time.

A breath, a verberation, a certain chord struck
on the strings that bind our faith to dream.

III.   Poetry can repair no loss, but it defies the space which separates.

I am happy with long silence,
with the rattle of the wind,
happy to let go unspoken
all that's sweet and rests between us
like water in the boll of the great hollow halftree
on the side of the sundusted roadway.
         I drink deep.

Let the parched hearts caterwaul,
haul transient tomes
         inscribed with borrowed sorrows,
bask in longings not their own,
the ardors no one dares pursue—
         or even utter—
as if hungry for the torture,
the silence of the names they dare not speak,
the floodtide growing deep
as each thought drops relentless,
         irretrievable,
into the darker chambers of the heart
until the day the heart has no choice
         but to burst.

Pity as well the oblivious ones
who live in swells of wrong words,
forever the wrong words spilling forth,
all those ill-begotten words,
filling every silence in and out
with chatter and amnesia,
with the hollowest of calls.

This is no way to go through the wood.

I may be no tracker but I know:
the wood does not need you
      or me
         to be its muse.

For that it has the dry leaves and the snow
and snowmelt's raucous rivulets,
quick fur between the birches' silver trunks,
a hundred other minuscule unfoldings,
a thousand stirrings we will never know.

We left this home as soon as we chose
to make our living dealing meanings.
We are guests here now.
Wise ones stick to paths
the world has left us.
Wise ones speak when spoken to.
We are neither wind nor river
nor burnished river stones.
We cast ourselves out.
I am certain of it now.
We must carry our home
in our heart as we circle
and circle in search of
the heart of the world.

So this is how it goes.

You and I together, here,
are all the center we will ever have,
the center we've been circling all along,
the crystalline core within the stone,
the epicenter of the quake,
the eye of every storm that's carved
its path across the plains,
the caesura in a startled breath,

whatever sets the aspen leaves to tremble,
the last red gleam in a dying ember,
the way waves leave their signature in sand,
the way life carves itself into the palm of every hand.

3. SPRUNG

The silence is not suppression; instead, it is all there is.
—Annie Dillard, *Teaching a Stone to Talk: Encounters and Expeditions*

A Reminder

You were busy making masks
for no body in particular to wear
and the walls were staring at you,
all unblinking fixtures, while I
contemplated how to change my hair,
change it like so many clothes.
(I don't like being a girl like this;
it happens only when I am bored.)
I was wearing a shirt of yours,
flannel and down to my knees.

The stove glowed with persistence
and for once we were warm together.
As if breaking a promise
we embraced the comfort of fire,
watched it leap and gambol
as if another living creature
we have taken on, taken in,
though really, it possesses us,
like your many faces possess you
and create you. What it means
to be what are widely called artists:
We belong to each other
only briefly and breathlessly:
the erasure of solitude surprises us.

Cheeks flushed, we tend one another
like fires, eyes drawn inexorably
toward the other's movements,
the flickers and signals
speaking those most intimate of truths,
indecipherable to those who would look on.

Your masks are more transparent,
their rage, delight, surprise more pure
than day-to-day shadows
cast by day-to-day flames,
more pure than my words—
forever circling all that you capture so quick.
Who lives deeper in the heart of the real?
And why must I keep asking?

Comparisons strip away the meat,
suck out the marrow and leave us
like paper, flat, dried and partial,
awaiting the fire. Our only hope
of completion is in the ashes, the dust,
the return to the unshifting forms.
I hope to speak less, but hope
wastes the heart, makes it brittle
and bitter, a shell of itself,
with no core. Breath comes in sighs,
sings its frustration with words
that will never speak true.

You go on tracing and trimming,
you embrace approximation,
while I add layer upon layer
and line upon line, feeling some
shiver of need to brace myself,
to insulate. Watching you,
I feel my own art stifle and pale,
I feel it move farther and farther away.

If I could be more fleeting,
relearn the brief and breathless,
quit drifting into theory, into form,
my body might know, if I let it,
how to be, how to set itself warm.

For Sappho

If not, winter will catch you—
    so sing.

Sing woman about whom nothing is known.

Sing with your head thrown back,
your hair a stormtossed flock,
open your throat naked to the sky and its knives.

Before the wind, sing now.
Before it takes your breath,
leaves your skin chipped and pitted,
dry as leaves before the first snow,
before it cracks clean your bones.

Winter lays itself blind and white.
All slows. Something whispers,
Do not move stones.

The foundation shifts.
Ice settles its sheets.
Sing woman, sing now,
while snow engulfs all breath.
Comes in clouds, coldest now—
it's at its coldest caught
between darkest night and hungry thaw—
the lilac hour before your death
when ring songs sweeter than sun on skin.

And if not spring will hold you, woman,
still some winter will,
all crystalline, in truth, your kin—
    so sing.

Taking Notes: Cold Comfort

The cows stand
exactly where you left them.
The jersey's purple slug tongue
reaches for your hand.
Only the whitetailed does move,
browsing fogflung groves
and bolting at your footfall,
at your breath.

Not a bird calls. January.
The sun, when it comes,
hits at odd gaunt angles.
Your projects are no longer yours.
You've shuffled and shunted
your belongings—your belonging—
so many times, you've learned
to keep the important stuff
well-hidden, salient chaos,
delicious morass.

Come night, the wind
will clear the fog out.
Wind does not look back.

Someday you will go down
to the forlorn brown field
and build a fire there of brush
and cherrywood and birch.

For now, watch chimneys breathe,
heat rippling against bare hills.
The road raises clouds
you thought at first were fog.
It's dustier than January should be.

An owl slaloms through spruces.
Black dog at the mailbox ambles home.
The everpresent hum of man too much to bear.
Ash and dust gather on sparse snow.

Someday you will find
a ledge grown over
with juniper and vetch.
Into it you'll build
an earthen house
and keep your fire there.

STILL SNOW

A tough patchy crust but the crocuses
and robins do not mind. There is enough
sun in the soil to survive. Winter
asks what we will burn, what we'll keep alive.
Spring finds what will take root and what will fly.
Holed up in darker corners of the earth
the dead, or so we think, remain unmoved
by new light as it filters through the trees'
new budded shoots. But, oh, how rooted things
do move! The sweetly buried come to me
by dream. By dream I build my garden here,
wait for the snow to sink, for buried life
to blast the crust, to rise and drink the sky.
Oh, how my lips would take that clear cold wine!

Between Winter and Spring

I.

Owl outside the window—
listen close—the low sound
of hope—approaching snow—
and knowing I am home.

II.

You and I, we've always been a garden.
What sunlight I can muster, I will share
as long as you provide some solid soil.
You are welcome to the downy hours
of my dawn, if only you will open
up an evening now and then, or else a
redgold afternoon with all the tulips
blooming. What I love most is the long thaw,
the way each day stretches its tips, sunlight
pulled wider, slightly, than the day before.
Surely we will weather months more bitter,
of implacable greys, air thin as lace.
The cold is not so daunting anymore.
I have lived the myth of snow on cedars
against the holiness of frozen lakes
where nothing ever goes anonymous.
A revelation, this steady delight
in the earth as it is, its diligence.
Call it a little carriage of the soul.

III.

When the moon is whole—
a second sun—
the sky grows lighter
as it rises.
Closer than a ghost,
your hand meets mine.
Soon there will be snow.
There will be time.
We need not unearth
our surfaces.

Eight White Tulips

Eight white tulips he gave to me.
I gave them an old glass bottle,
its label advertising milk.
The cat has nibbled daintily
at the petals, now not so pure,
with toothpocked scars like slubs in silk.
I change the water when it grimes
to a translucent olive murk.
Already the leaf tips are browned and
incurled, a witches' fingernails.
Some may intimate an omen,
declare to me, all blossoms wilt—
I know better. I am corners
occupied at last. I'm soft claws
clasping, and I am soft claws clasped.
We do not need to bury roots.
Decay slinks in at its own pace.
The cat I will let masticate.
A white tulip is a tulip.
Advice is detritus and fringe.
I've never held a phantom hand
and gardens are not grown by ghosts.

Monadnock

I. Ascent

We walk a high road, you and I,
across wide swathes of open stone
where one finds the veins of the earth exposed.
Not once have we fallen.

To only know the earth vicariously
would be a tragedy akin
to never knowing it at all.

Words must not make more than half your life.

We have dreamed of being peregrines.
Wingless as we are, the world may teach us yet
to sail across this sheerest face.
If anybody, you and I will do it, and with grace.

Let us celebrate the partings and meetings of flexible beings
in places where one may tap the veins
or simply breathe the smell of everything.

If my words sound to you
like Emerson—Dillard—Whitman—
Snyder—Oliver—Thoreau—
it is not because—not just because—
I've read their words and feign to know
some fraction of those souls.
We've walked the same bald ridgelines,
felt the pulse below,
and try, forever falling short,

to set that song in static ink
so that someone else might go
to seek these things so purely felt,
impossible to show.

II. On the way down

I met three sisters on the mountain.
They were whitehaired and strong
in the way small women are
who have lived long in this world
and know right well their part of it.
We shared nods and hello.
From their wellworn smiles I could tell
there is art in growing old.

On Being the Forgotten One

I read poems today until I struck one that made me cry.

It was Pablo Neruda,
Si tu me olvidas—
>*If you forget me.*

This time it's not the closing lines,
dulzura implacable,
>not that declaration of implacable sweetness,
>relentless love,

but the middle stanzas that feel real.

I'm left standing alone on the shore of the heart,
>*mis raices,*
>*my roots trembling*
>>as you sail away.

I'm fighting the impulse to call out,
>*no me dejas,*
>*no me olvidas,*

knowing there's no use,

no use in calling out to far stone cliffs—
>they toss all words back, hollowed—

and knowing, too, that it feels good
giving voice,
>giving breath,
>>to this lopsided love that won't let go.

I breathe until it hurts.

Seeing you crest the horizon, I smile—
       flight or return?

Every return a flight
and every flight return.
I know now I am not your home.

Better uprooted on my own shore,
       better extinguished,
            eternally lost,
than waterlogged,
      sunk,
            algae and rust.

So I'm wandering the wreckage,
       lingering a while on my devastated shore,
       limp and flattened,
waiting for a fresh breeze
to come and clear me,
         even if it cannot carry me.

I know better than to run.

I'm over love,
      I'm over falling,
           over running somewhere new
           again to fall.

Dulzura implacable:
sweetness ruthless,
        sweetness cruel,
I'm over it all.

Leave me with *la rama roja*,
        the red branch
        and the crystal moon.
No me busques.

The just-so love never offers itself
to those who run off,
        set sail after it.

A root above the sand and soil,
dulzura trips me—
                we all know this—
when I'm not looking out for it,
        grabs me by the ankle
               just as I'm letting go.

Said the Explorer to the Settler

Remember that one sunset through the naked birches,
coral fire thrumming, great heart slowing into dusk?

Remember the dragfooted salamander emerging
nimbletailed and askew, up from the loam,
head all bobbled with the scattering sun?

Remember the arcane curve of the snail,
husked out for eternity on the mantle,
captured shadow reckoning its own depth?

Remember that stray garlic skin
    I tried to give to you last night,
its curve cupped and perched so delicate over your curls?
Remember the song I tried to sing to you?
How the words writhed their way out, larval, as I slept?
Now they've wings, now they've gone.

Remember the loam and remember the bones
which grow slower than leaves.
Remember the grey tangled path through the trees.
Remember the bulbs that I planted,
    the vast months we waited,
lonely and windswept, the freeze and the splinter, the thaw,
the freeze again, the splinter, and the thaw,
the bone deep knowing none of this is flaw:
the blackshackled crow song, the ramshackle geese,
field of turkey scattered, bedraggled as spring sheep.
Time to put away the old wool, gather up the new.

Remember best everything I cannot give to you.
I've been thinking bird thoughts,
plucking at what's writhing and what's drying.
This day now a drought,
the sort that shrivels not body
but soul and its seeds.

Thinking bird thoughts today, and lovers' thoughts,
trudging summer's longlost weeds;
thinking thoughts more dream than thought,
wishing they'd bring me some wings;
thinking nightdappled sidewalks that pull me home
wordless and wayward and wanton—
home where I gather up armfuls of you,
lap mouthfuls of you—O lovely!—
hold my hips and bite my lips!
Don't mince your minutes,
do not lose your grip.

What we've cobbled here, a most remarkable domestic.
Let's pitch our stones and break the windows
    while the wind is from the south.
Thicker velvet's on the way, you feel it? Hear it—
listen to the rock doves' throats,
    the rock doves on the nextdoor porch.
Let's listen from this temporary patch of sun, mud, grass;
let's set a while in the borrowed chairs;
    let's soak up here and now
while we tap the sweet escapist in our makeup
and gather all the leaves worth taking.

I've tomorrow in the crosshairs, quick—
pack up the wagon, untangle the map, the one you drew
    with the road that leads all ways to every where.
Come pioneer, forget that wagon, grab your pack,
it's high time we turned pilgrim.

MAY

> and we had to train our sights on her
> as commonplace as some endangered species can seem.
> —James Tate, "A New Beginning"

I.

May's signature,
despite its sprout
       bud
              bloom,
has always been
       departure
       and decay.

Welcome, the end of beginnings!
Welcome, the first pearls of stagnation!

Hearts emerge from hibernation
       stircrazy,
          smell the salt breeze
or the lack of it
       and leave
            or feel they ought.

II.

This spring thaw merely the season of delayed decay:
death happening after the fact, cut short, frozen midway
by that harsh mistress winter. I need a haircut.

Still skipping stones, still skipping classes,
adolescing into corpulence, distortion—
perhaps both—
friendless, unmothered, woefully verbose,
abandoned by those homes
from which we strove so long to loose ourselves,
we totter toward form without substance,
reason without argument.

If we go inching across the bleak beaches of childhood,
into tawdry forests long untrodden,
cut through the mayhem of succession,
generations edging into loam,
will we wield once more
our driftwood javelin and sword?

Our first year no longer saplings:
less malleable now and no longer so lithe.
I still wish I were as long and tall and skinny as my shadow,
spread out along the broadlit field in the hours
just before the dusk, just after dawn.

Such form once seemed plausible,
back in the days when we swallowed
wholeheartedly, heart and whole,
the myths of resistance,
back when we lived on histories,
back when we verged on ether,
before we bartered away the old wishes
for hot food and cold steel.

III.

Misery of expenditure:
endless rotation of replacement parts,
life to excess a mere echo of death.

Misery of metaphor:
words no longer tangible as they were
when we lapped up our mothers' fairy tales.

Misery of migrants:
the mercenary poor with nothing left
to give but another weary hour,
fibers stretched to just this side of snapping.

IV.

We lose childhood to politics
as we lose our homes to the weather.
Such erosions cut too near the heart
for any human hands to measure.

V.

If not build a house,
I'd like at least
to pitch a tent with you.

Dreams filled with clay and iron,
pots on the fire, woolen socks
and songs for supper.

I wake with a start after sunset
and the rain is gone.

The walking is best when it's dark.
Even waking, even walking,
days later I can taste your salt.
The wind picks up, 10:00 pm or so
and I am never cold, not anymore.

So I stand on the hill with my face to the lake
counting fireflies, imagining
their bedraggled wings as they blink their way
through damp grass to their others.

Morning comes quicker, brighter:
watch the swallows,
only gravity the choicest gnats,
the daintiest twigs.

Frightful this impulse
to settle, to nest.
No longer a guest to myself,
I am setting up shop in this notion:
say happiness is a place,
something you and I could make.

And if we build our happiness,
it will be well-proportioned,
with a cellar and a skylight
and a cold, sweet spring.
And if we've space and sun and soil,
there will be a garden.
I will learn to grow sweet potatoes
and so many kinds of garlic.
And if there are sheep,
I will knit, I will weave
until the time we've been keeping
no longer means.

And if—and if—and if—
this restless pulse of mine
propels each day away from hesitation,
sets each foot in front of the other
toward this most mundane of loves.
My words are too utilitarian today
for what silk wishes it could be.

VI.

Cold, hard buds
       of the new season:
iceless at last
       we toss aside logic,
spit reason out
between our teeth
to see whose shoots
       the farthest.

O, my few
and far between!
We've fallen farther
       from the tree
than did our fathers
       and we're growing
into sturdy things,
       wellspined and more mythic
       than we could have dreamed.

VII.

A cave, a nest,
a hollowed log,
a spit of sand,
a patch of grass
that stretches tall
above our heads:
we are at home
and wander slow.
We're so at home
we disappear
into the long light
and the shadows
cast by branches,
cast by grasses,
by our own long limbs.

It has no end, this song!
I can't pin our beginning!
So this is some eternal spring,
some well that will never, has never
run dry. It's May now, and May splits the sky.

ON NOMADISM

The nomad is stable only when experiencing velocity.
Movement is a matter not of toward but of through.
What we leave behind is never a straight line.
Feet are not bricks and even bones have curves.
She longs for dirt roads. Pavement kills the knees.

They tell her, *Stick to the main streets girlie,* hija,
don't push your luck on the backroads,
they'll take things you didn't know you had.
She shrugs them a smile and shoulders her load
and she doesn't once look back.

She's started feeling tiny vibrations,
like a cell phone ringing with the sound turned off,
through the feet, in the shoulders,
along the xylophone of ribs,
and she casts about for a call, a message.

Spain, July

I. Twenty-Five Days

The ants
and the flies
love more than
anything
the sweet salt
blisters
on my feet.

II. What I Carry

Wild mint and sorrel,
dill and chamomile,
fourleaf *tréboles,*
palabras:
always something
in my mouth.

III. The Most

What I miss the most:
wild black raspberries.

IV. Hilltop

How quickly the city
turns into the middle
of nowhere! Vice versa.

V. Sense Memory

Mineral savor
of sunscreen,
mineral savor
of sweat.
Everyday
is camphor cream,
coffee, cigarettes.

VI. Purity

Clean, unclean:
a matter of degree.

Dead Tree

The north wants you.
The west wants you.
The east wants you.
You hunger for here—

this southernmost of islands
in the smallest of counties,
this pettiest of skirmishes
in the thorniest of families.

All you asked was raspberry and wave,
rock decked with fossils   all they gave:
a patch, a hesitation, low snarl,
fire doused—a hiss.

Leave the smoke behind you,
trailing, bittering the air.
Your difference is this:
let go, sink noiseless,
tap the silence,
simmer,
boil it.

Your sweetness is
a longdrawn labor,
comes but once a year.

Unsure of roots,
eternity,
you drag your feet
through sand and ask

what to do,
where to go,
whether to go
and what the weather—

What do you bring?
And how do you leave
the cold
        the dry
                the tumbledown
behind?

Lost among promise and conspiracy,
lost without love,
        you are lost,
the only map the series
of tactical maneuvers
it takes to live here,
        to survive.

Hum like the sky,
electric, hesitant,
unleash yourself at last
and split the trunk,
dive deeper than the roots,
forget the difference
between trees
        and water.
Forge yourself,
thunder's daughter.

This is kindling.
This your fire.

Feed something other than your wounds
with something other than your tears.

None can outwait miracles.
Few can outwit stars—
first maps, dying waves, impossible shores,
strange wakes to stretch so far.

Promise yourself you will not marry
your future
                or your past.
If you must wed,
      wed not the moment
      nor the idea of the moment,
but movement itself,
and only if you must.

Marry fury,
marry the taste
of salt and iron
in your blood.

Leave behind time,
its passage your wake,
stare into the sun, forsake
all that refuses to vanish.

Choose distance.
Choose the smallest and lightest
      of kindnesses.
Abandon even language.

The ridgeline, the road:
      the only home.
Hold what's farthest,
      hold it close.

Spinoza Poem #2

I possess the will to color,
you possess the will to line.
With our hands joined, sweet tracer,
we will craft ourselves a life.

It will not be a life of longing
nor a shifting life of time.
We will stretch it, bold and infinite,
along an axis with no name.

And you will call me joy
and I'll call you the same
and we will know the truth of it,
its nature and its name.

Not our joining but our passage
is love's kindle and its flame.
I see it every morning,
our passage in your eyes:

reflection of the sun just risen,
tempering the night.
Its circle is our path, carved heaven:
this our color, this our line.

And love is but one shape joy takes,
one of several shades.
Joy lies not in what we have.
It lives in what we make.

Digging

You split the skin of it, the earth, and waited
for an answer to pour forth, a song to rise
a wraith, a wisp, a slip of smoke dust,
meet your lungs halfway and give your voice
the words it thirsts, lusts, starves itself of body
in order to utter the truth some say will set you free.
Back to the soil—you've sweated and sobbed
every drop of what keeps you alive;
your breath won't even cloud the cold,
and still too big, your breath, too strange its shapes,
for any other body's lungs. You've mined the hills,
the villagers, their songs, and still no closer
to an explanation, to a settlement, the home
you promised to your body—for its limbs
to take a break—or else your body promised you
someday to cease its motions, fickle, futile:
end the dance and leave you to your tattered,
lonely song, the feral frequencies of mind
without its matter, oh, this lonely task,
too much to ask, the music, molten,
humming up through roots—the earth's
imaginary miracle and interference all too real,
no hope alone can dig you out the hole
you helped to open up with sharded shovel,
rusted blade, hands querulous with fragile age
anticipated: years to come consume you.
Your futurity your chain to now,
the hole you dug how many years ago,
the life you're losing by the moment over moment,
blink and breath of waking, breath and blink
of sleep takes reins you thought had rotted

out along the path: abandoned dreams
and cobblestones all half-submerged,
your distant past that tried for bright
and failed to meet your future buried headlong.
Now you're hungry and you're cynical,
and waiting for a miracle to replace the loves
you lost, forgot and left for dead, the neckdeep burials,
the dreams you lay, ruined bouquets
alongside burntout castoff bodies,
char, decay. Skin is never skin for long
but song is song is song is song.

Because You Were Not Home

Because you were not home
I went down to the rocks
and watched small fish
nose and hop, surface
for their supper, for the dusk.

Because you were not home
I went down to the sand
and skipped five flat stones,
watched each ripple out,
making circles of the slenderest of lights.

The moon waited, crescent,
behind the highest branches.
Time circled, circled
silent in my pocket,
tracing its own wake.

I rested on rocks
that twenty years ago were boulders.
Twenty years makes every thing smaller
except the water. The water
stretches out farther and farther.

Fomite
Burlington, Vermont

Fomite is a literary press whose authors and artists explore the human condition — political, cultural, personal and historical — in poetry and prose.

A fomite is a medium capable of transmitting infectious organisms from one individual to another.

"The activity of art is based on the capacity of people to be infected by the feelings of others." Tolstoy, *What is Art?*

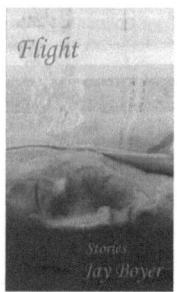

Flight and Other Stories - Jay Boyer
In *Flight and Other Stories*, we're with the fattest woman on earth as she draws her last breaths and her soul ascends toward its final reward. We meet a divorcee who can fly for no more effort than flapping her arms. We follow a middle-aged butler whose love affair with a young woman leads him first to the mysteries of bondage, and then to the pleasures of malice. Story by story, we set foot into worlds so strange as to seem all but surreal, yet everything feels familiar, each moment rings true. And that's when we recognize we're in the hands of one of America's truly original talents.

AlphaBetaBestiario - Antonello Borra
Animals have always understood that mankind is not fully at home in the world. Bestiaries, hoping to teach, send out warnings. This one, of course, aims at doing the same.

Loisaida - Dan Chodorokoff
Catherine, a young anarchist estranged from her parents and squatting in an abandoned building on New York's Lower East Side is fighting with her boyfriend and conflicted about her work on an underground newspaper. After learning of a developer's plans to demolish a community garden, Catherine builds an alliance with a group of Puerto Rican community activists. Together they confront the confluence of politics, money, and real estate that rule Manhattan. All the while she learns important lessons from her great-grandmother's life in the Yiddish anarchist movement that flourished on the Lower East Side at the turn of the century. In this coming of age story, family saga, and tale of urban politics, Dan Chodorkoff explores the "principle of hope", and examines how memory and imagination inform social change.

Fomite
Burlington, Vermont

Still Time - Michael Cocchiarale

Still Time is a collection of twenty-five short and shorter stories exploring tensions that arise in a variety of contemporary relationships: a young boy must deal with the wrath of his out-of-work father; a woman runs into a man twenty years after an awkward sexual encounter; a wife, unable to conceive, imagines her own murder, as well as the reaction of her emotionally distant husband; a soon-to-be tenured English professor tries to come to terms with her husband's shocking return to the religion of his youth; an assembly line worker, married for thirty years, discovers the surprising secret life of his recently hospitalized wife. Whether a few hundred or a few thousand words, these and other stories in the collection depict characters at moments of deep crisis. Some feel powerless, overwhelmed—unable to do much to change the course of their lives. Others rise to the occasion and, for better or for worse, say or do the thing that might transform them for good. Even in stories with the most troubling of endings, there remains the possibility of redemption. For each of the characters, there is still time.

Improvisational Arguments - Anna Faktorovich

Improvisational Arguments is written in free verse to capture the essence of modern problems and triumphs. The poems clearly relate short, frequently humorous and occasionally tragic, stories about travels to exotic and unusual places, fantastic realms, abnormal jobs, artistic innovations, political objections, and misadventures with love.

The Listener Aspires to the Condition of Music - Barry Goldensohn

"I know of no other selected poems that selects on one theme, but this one does, charting Goldensohn's career-long attraction to music's performance, consolations and its august, thrilling, scary and clownish charms. Does all art aspire to the condition of music as Pater claimed, exhaling in a swoon toward that one class act? Goldensohn is more aware than the late 19th century of the overtones of such breathing: his poems thoroughly round out those overtones in a poet's lifetime of listening."

John Peck, poet, editor, Fellow of the American Academy of Rome

Fomite
Burlington, Vermont

When You Remember Deir Yassin - R.L Green

When You Remember Deir Yassin is a collection of poems by R. L. Green, an American Jewish writer, on the subject of the occupation and destruction of Palestine. Green comments: "Outspoken Jewish critics of Israeli crimes against humanity have, strangely, been called "anti-Semitic" as well as the hilariously illogical epithet "self-hating Jews." As a Jewish critic of the Israeli government, I have come to accept these accusations as a stamp of approval and a badge of honor, signifying my own fealty to a central element of Jewish identity and ethics: one must be a lover of truth and a friend to the oppressed, and stand with the victims of tyranny, not with the tyrants, despite tribal loyalty or self-advancement. These poems were written as expressions of outrage, and of grief, and to encourage my sisters and brothers of every cultural or national grouping to speak out against injustice, to try to save Palestine, and in so doing, to reclaim for myself my own place as part of the Jewish people. The poems are offered in the original English with Arabic and Hebrew translations accompanying each poem.

The Co-Conspirator's Tale - Ron Jacobs

There's a place where love and mistrust are never at peace; where duplicity and deceit are the universal currency. *The Co-Conspirator's Tale* takes place within this nebulous firmament. There are crimes committed by the police in the name of the law. Excess in the name of revolution. The combination leaves death in its wake and the survivors struggling to find justice in a San Francisco Bay Area noir by the author of the underground classic *The Way the Wind Blew: A History of the Weather Underground* and the novel *Short Order Frame Up*.

Roadworthy Creature, Roadworthy Craft - Kate Magill

Words fail but the voice struggles on. The culmination of a decade's worth of performance poetry, *Roadworthy Creature, Roadworthy Craft* is Kate Magill's first full-length publication. In lines that are sinewy yet delicate, Magill's poems explore the terrain where idea and action meet, where bodies and words commingle to form a strange new flesh, a breathing text, an "I" that spirals outward from itself.

Fomite
Burlington, Vermont

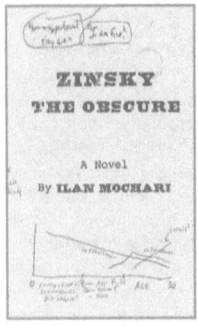

Zinsky the Obscure - Ilan Mochari

"If your childhood is brutal, your adulthood becomes a daily attempt to recover: a quest for ecstasy and stability in recompense for their early absence." So states the 30-year-old Ariel Zinsky, whose bachelor-like lifestyle belies the torturous youth he is still coming to grips with. As a boy, he struggles with the beatings themselves; as a grownup, he struggles with the world's indifference to them. *Zinsky the Obscure* is his life story, a humorous chronicle of his search for a redemptive ecstasy through sex, an entrepreneurial sports obsession, and finally, the cathartic exercise of writing it all down. Fervently recounting both the comic delights and the frightening horrors of a life in which he feels – always – that he is not like all the rest, Zinsky survives the worst and relishes the best with idiosyncratic style, as his heartbreak turns into self-awareness and his suicidal ideation into self-regard. A vivid evocation of the all-consuming nature of lust and ambition – and the forces that drive them – *Zinsky the Obscure* is a novel of extraordinary zeal, range, and power.

The Derivation of Cowboys & Indians - Joseph D. Reich

The Derivation of Cowboys & Indians represents a profound journey, a breakdown of The American Dream from a social, cultural, historical, and spiritual point of view. Reich examines in concise detail the loss of the collective unconscious, commenting on our!contemporary postmodern culture with its self-interested excesses, on where and how things all go wrong, and how social/political practice rarely meets its original proclamations and promises. Reich's surreal and! self-effacing satire brings this troubling message home. *The Derivations of Cowboys & Indians* is a desperate!search and struggle for America's literal, symbolic, and spiritual home.

Kasper Planet: Comix and Tragix - Peter Schumann

The British call him Punch, the Italians, Pulchinello, the Russians, Petruchka, the Native Americans, Coyote. These are the figures we may know. But every culture that worships authority will breed a Punch-like, anti-authoritan resister. Yin and yang -- it has to happen. The Germans call him Kasper.
Truth-telling and serious pranking are dangerous professions when going up against power. Bradley Manning sits naked in solitary; Julian Assange is pursued by Interpol, Obama's Department of Justice, and Amazon.com. But -- in contrast to merely human faces -- masks and theater can often slip through the bars.
Consider our American Kaspers: Charlie Chaplin, Woody Guthrie, Abby Hoffman, the Yes Men -- theater people all, utilizing various forms to seed critique. Their profiles and tactics have evolved along with those of their enemies.
Who are the bad guys that call forth the Kaspers? Over the last half century, with his Bread & Puppet Theater, Peter Schumann has been tireless in naming them, excoriating them with Kasperdom....
from Marc Estrin's Foreword to Planet Kasper

Fomite
Burlington, Vermont

Views Cost Extra - L.E. Smith

Views that inspire, that calm, or that terrify – all come at some cost to the viewer. In *Views Cost Extra* you will find a New Jersey high school preppy who wants to inhabit the "perfect" cowboy movie, a rural mailman disgusted with the residents of his town who wants to live with the penguins, an ailing screen writer who strikes a deal with Johnny Cash to reverse an old man's failures, an old man who ponders a young man's suicide attempt, a one-armed blind blues singer who wants to reunite with the car that took her arm on the assembly line — and more. These stories suggest that we must pay something to live even ordinary lives.

The Empty Notebook Interrogates Itself - Susan Thomas

The Empty Notebook began its life as a very literal metaphor for a few weeks of what the poet thought was writer's block, but was really the struggle of an eccentric persona to take over her working life. It won. And for the next three years everything she wrote came to her in the voice of the Empty Notebook, who, as the notebook began to fill itself, became rather opinionated, changed gender, alternately acted as bully and victim, had many bizarre adventures in exotic locales and developed a somewhat politically-incorrect attitude. It then began to steal the voices and forms of other poets and tried to immortalize itself in various poetry reviews. It is now thrilled to collect itself in one slim volume.

My God, What Have We Done? - Susan Weiss

In a world afflicted with war, toxicity, and hunger, does what we do in our private lives really matter? Fifty years after the creation of the atomic bomb at Los Alamos, newlyweds Pauline and Clifford visit that once-secret city on their honeymoon, compelled by Pauline's fascination with Oppenheimer, the soulful scientist. The two stories emerging from this visit reverberate back and forth between the loneliness of a new mother at home in Boston and the isolation of an entire community dedicated to the development of the bomb. While Pauline struggles with unforeseen challenges of family life, Oppenheimer and his crew reckon with forces beyond all imagining.

Finally the years of frantic research on the bomb culminate in a stunning test explosion that echoes a rupture in the couple's marriage. Against the backdrop of a civilization that's out of control, Pauline begins to understand the complex, potentially explosive physics of personal relationships.

At once funny and dead serious, *My God, What Have We Done?* sifts through the ruins left by the bomb in search of a more worthy human achievement.

www.ingramcontent.com/pod-product-compliance
Lightning Source LLC
Chambersburg PA
CBHW031255290426
44109CB00012B/590